THE C.E.O.'S LITTLE INSTRUCTION BOOK

Presented By
Van Crouch Communications, Inc.

The C.E.O.'s Little Instruction Book
ISBN 1-57757-009-X

Copyright © 1996 by Trade Life Books, Inc.

Published by Trade Life Books, Inc.
P. O. Box 55325
Tulsa, Oklahoma 74155

Presented by *Van Crouch Communications, Inc.*
P. O. Box 320
Wheaton, Illinois 60189

INTRODUCTION

They're men and women of influence and persuasion. You rarely know what they're thinking. But you wish you did! You infrequently get an audience with them. But you wish you could!

They're called "Big-wigs," "Moneymakers," "Controversial, "Successful." Yet, they're ordinary human beings like you and me who decided to risk the extraordinary — and prevailed.

Now with *The C.E.O.'s Little Instruction Book* you can have access to the inner chamber of these exceptional executive minds! Packed into this little pocketbook is the creativity, genius, inspiration, and talent which have taken these successful men and women from the cubicle to the corner office.

Learn of their passions and their purposes — their fervor to live lives set apart, to rise above the daily struggles with resilience, to make a distinctive difference.

The road to success is always under construction.

JOHN W. PATTEN
Former Publisher
BUSINESS WEEK MAGAZINE

[JOHN PATTEN'S SUCCESSFUL CAREER WITH MCGRAW-HILL
SUBSEQUENTLY ALLOWED HIM TO BECOME PUBLISHER OF *BUSINESS WEEK*.
UNDER PATTEN'S GUIDANCE, *BUSINESS WEEK* EXPANDED ITS READERSHIP
TO OVER ONE MILLION, LAUNCHED THREE FOREIGN-LANGUAGE EDITIONS,
AND WON THE INDUSTRY'S HIGHEST HONOR.]

One who never asks either knows everything or nothing.

MALCOLM FORBES, SR.

Former Chairman
FORBES MAGAZINE

[MALCOLM FORBES, SR. INHERITED *FORBES MAGAZINE* FROM HIS FATHER AND BUILT IT INTO A SUCCESSFUL BUSINESS WITH OVER A HALF MILLION SUBSCRIBERS.]

To me, it's very simple; if you're going to be thinking anyway, you might as well think big.

DONALD TRUMP

Chairman
TRUMP ORGANIZATION

[DONALD TRUMP STARTED IN BUSINESS AS A DEVELOPER IN NEW YORK CITY. HE IS CURRENTLY A SELF-MADE BILLIONAIRE, WITH ASSETS IN EXCESS OF A BILLION DOLLARS.]

*Nothing in the world can take the place
of persistence....*

• • •

*The quality of an individual is reflected in the
standards they set for themselves.*

RAY KROC

Former Chairman
MCDONALD'S

[RAY FOUNDED THE FAST FOOD INDUSTRY WITH MCDONALD'S, BUILDING IT WITH A CONTINUAL
EMPHASIS ON AUTOMATION AND STANDARDIZATION OF OPERATIONS. TODAY, MCDONALD'S IS THE
INTERNATIONAL ICON OF THE FAST FOOD INDUSTRY.]

*The world stands on its head
...for those few and far between
souls who devote 100 percent.*

ANDREW CARNEGIE

Founder
CARNEGIE STEEL COMPANY

[CARNEGIE STARTED HIS WORKING CAREER IN A COTTON FACTORY, WENT
ON TO WORK FOR A TELEGRAPH OFFICE AND SUBSEQUENTLY FOR THE
PENNSYLVANIA RAILROAD. HE FOUNDED SEVERAL STEEL MILLS,
EVENTUALLY CONSOLIDATING HIS VAST HOLDINGS INTO THE CARNEGIE
STEEL COMPANY.]

*Success is a journey,
not a destination.*

JOSEPH GORMAN

Chairman
TRW, INC.

[JOSEPH'S CAREER IN THE AUTO INDUSTRY BEGAN NOT LONG AFTER HIS
GRADUATION FROM YALE. WITH JOSEPH AT THE HELM, TRW IS
CURRENTLY ONE OF THE MAJOR AUTO PARTS SUPPLIERS TO
DETROIT'S BIG THREE.]

Great achievement is usually born of great sacrifice, and is never the result of selfishness.

NAPOLEON HILL

Founder
NAPOLEON HILL ASSOCIATES

[ANDREW CARNEGIE GAVE HILL, AT THE AGE OF TWENTY-FIVE, A UNIQUE AND LENGTHY ASSIGNMENT: RESEARCH AND INTERVIEW THE NATION'S MOST SUCCESSFUL MEN TO FIND A SUCCESS FORMULA. HILL'S FIRST PUBLISHED WORK, BASED ON THIS ASSIGNMENT, LATER EVOLVED INTO HIS MOST FAMOUS WORK, *THINK AND GROW RICH*.]

Nothing can be accomplished until you begin.

• • •

Success is much more quickly
attained when you expect it.

IRA HAYES

Manager
Advertising Department
NCR CORPORATION

[IRA'S MANY SUCCESSES WITH NCR CAUSED HIS PROMOTION TO HEAD OF ADVERTISING AND
ORGANIZER OF THE SPEAKER'S BUREAU. HE IS WIDELY RECOGNIZED AS THE "AMBASSADOR OF
ENTHUSIASM" AND AS AN AUTHORITY ON POSITIVE THINKING AND MOTIVATIONAL BEHAVIOR.]

Genius is 1 percent inspiration and 99 percent perspiration.

THOMAS A. EDISON

Inventor and Founder
EDISON ELECTRIC LIGHT COMPANY

[ALTHOUGH EDISON IS KNOWN FOR MANY INVENTIONS, HIS GREATEST CONTRIBUTION IS THE FIRST ELECTRIC LIGHT POWER STATION. ITS TREMENDOUS SUCCESS LED TO THE FOUNDING OF EDISON ELECTRIC LIGHT COMPANY, WHICH LATER MERGED INTO THE GENERAL ELECTRIC COMPANY.]

All of life is the management of risk, not its elimination.

WALTER WRISTON

Former Chairman
CITICORP

[JOINING CITIBANK IN 1946, WRISTON WORKED HIS WAY UP IN THE CORPORATION'S U. S. AND FOREIGN STRUCTURE. HE WAS NAMED PRESIDENT CEO IN 1967, AND CHAIRMAN OF CITICORP IN 1970. WRISTON ALSO SERVES ON THE BOARDS OF GENERAL ELECTRIC, CHUBB, AND TANDEM.]

Never get discouraged and never quit. Because if you never quit, you're never beaten.

TED TURNER

Founder
TURNER BROADCASTING SYSTEM

[TED TURNER STARTED HIS EMPIRE WITH A BILLBOARD BUSINESS. HE USED IT TO BUY A FAILING TELEVISION STATION, WHICH HE TURNED INTO A GREAT SUCCESS. AS A RESULT, HE BOUGHT THE ATLANTA BRAVES, LAUNCHED CNN AND ACQUIRED MGM.]

...Most people get ahead during the time that others waste.

• • •

Failure is only the opportunity to begin again more intelligently.

HENRY FORD

Founder
FORD MOTOR COMPANY

[FORD WAS BORN ON A FARM NEAR DEARBORN, MICHIGAN. HE DISLIKED FARM LIFE BUT HAD A LOVE AND APTITUDE FOR MACHINERY. HIS EXPERIMENTATION RESULTED IN THE INVENTION OF THE FIRST MASS-PRODUCED CAR IN THE WORLD, THE MODEL T FORD AND THE FORD MOTOR COMPANY.]

You are the same today that you are going to be five years from now except for two things; the people...you associate, and the books you read.

CHARLES "TREMENDOUS" JONES

President
LIFE MANAGEMENT SERVICES, INC.

[CHARLIE JONES FOUNDED HIS OWN MANAGEMENT COMPANY THAT SPECIALIZES IN GIVING MANAGEMENT SEMINARS THROUGHOUT THE U. S. HE IS ALSO A RENOWNED WRITER AND SPEAKER.]

You can't run a business without taking risks.

MILLARD DREXLER

CEO
THE GAP

[DREXLER JOINED THE GAP IN 1983. HE IS CREDITED WITH SUCCESSFUL NEW CHAINS LIKE GAP-KIDS AND OLD NAVY, AND WITH MAJOR INPUT IN TRANSFORMING THE COMPANY INTO A PREMIER SPECIALTY RETAILER. WHEN GAP, INC.'S FOUNDER STEPPED DOWN IN SEPTEMBER, 1995, DREXLER SUCCEEDED HIM.]

No sale is really complete until the product is worn out, and the customer is satisfied.

LEON LEONWOOD BEAN

Founder

L. L. BEAN, INC.

[IN 1912, BEAN, AN AVID HUNTER AND FISHERMAN, CONCOCTED A HYBRID HUNTING BOOT. DECIDING TO SELL THE BOOTS BY MAIL, HE PROMISED FULL REFUNDS IF CUSTOMERS WEREN'T SATISFIED. NINETY OF HIS FIRST HUNDRED PAIRS FELL APART YET HE FULFILLED HIS GUARANTEE AND PERFECTED HIS PRODUCT. SETTING THE STANDARD BY WHICH L. L. BEAN, INC. CONTINUES TO THRIVE TODAY.]

Winners are just ex-losers who got mad.

• • •

You're not finished when you're defeated...
you're finished when you quit.

WILLIAM V. CROUCH

President
VAN CROUCH COMMUNICATIONS, INC.

[AFTER RANKING AS A CONSISTENT SALES LEADER WITH THE AMERICAN EXPRESS COMPANY, VAN
WENT ON TO RECEIVE MANY AWARDS FOR OUTSTANDING PERFORMANCE IN THE INSURANCE INDUSTRY
AND QUALIFIED AS A MEMBER OF THE MILLION DOLLAR ROUND TABLE. HE IS ONE OF
AMERICA'S MOST VERSATILE SPEAKERS.]

A man who trims himself to suit everybody will soon whittle himself away.

CHARLES SCHWAB

Former President
BETHLEHEM STEEL

[CHARLES STARTED WORK IN ANDREW CARNEGIE'S STEEL MILLS. HE WORKED HIS WAY UP INTO VARIOUS HIGH-LEVEL POSITIONS UNTIL HE WAS NAMED PRESIDENT OF CARNEGIE STEEL. HE BOUGHT BETHLEHEM STEEL COMPANY FROM ANDREW CARNEGIE AND EXPANDED HIS BUSINESS DURING WORLD WAR I.]

Do not fear mistakes. Wisdom is often born of...mistakes.

PAUL GALVIN

Founder
MOTOROLA

[IN THE 1930S PAUL FOUNDED MOTOROLA WITH THE IDEA OF MASS-PRODUCING CAR RADIOS. FROM THERE, HE CREATED SUCH PRODUCTS AS CELLULAR PHONES, PAGERS, AND SEMICONDUCTORS.]

The urge to quit is the last obstacle between you and your dreams.

RICHARD DeVOS

Co-founder and Former President
AMWAY CORPORATION

[RICH DeVOS, CO-FOUNDER OF AMWAY, ONE OF THE WORLD'S LARGEST PRIVATELY HELD COMPANIES, RECENTLY RETIRED AS PRESIDENT. HE IS AN ACCLAIMED AUTHOR AND SPEAKER.]

*Intellect doesn't determine success —
good choices do.*

• • •

Motivation comes from that which we value most.

JIM CATHCART

Former President
NATIONAL SPEAKERS' ASSOCIATION

[JIM IS THE FOUNDER OF A CONSULTING FIRM IN LA JOLLA, CALIFORNIA, AND A PARTNER IN A
PSYCHOLOGICAL RESEARCH FIRM IN CAREFREE, ARIZONA.]

The only place success comes before work is in the dictionary.

DONALD KENDALL

Former Chairman
PEPSICO

[ALTHOUGH DONALD KENDALL IS RETIRED, HE STILL DEVOTES TIME TO EXPANDING PEPSICO'S FAST FOOD INTERNATIONAL MARKET. HE IS ALSO THE CHAIRMAN OF A NEW INTERNATIONAL INVESTMENT FUND, RUNS TWO CATTLE RANCHES, AND HEADS THE NATIONAL FOREST FOUNDATION CONSERVATION GROUP.]

The only pretty store is the one full of people.

WILLIAM T. DILLARD

Founder
DILLARD'S DEPARTMENT STORES

[WILLIAM BEGAN HIS DREAM OF OWNING ONE OF THE COUNTRY'S LARGEST DEPARTMENT STORES WITH ONE STORE IN NASHVILLE, ARKANSAS. DILLARD'S PIONEERED THE USE OF ELECTRONIC CASH REGISTER AND COMPUTERIZED SYSTEMS, AND CURRENTLY GENERATES ANNUAL SALES IN THE NEIGHBORHOOD OF $4 BILLION.]

*My only business secret [is]...
to work harder than
everybody else.*

H. WAYNE HUIZENGA

Owner
MIAMI DOLPHINS

[BILLIONAIRE HUIZENGA, "THE MAN WITH THE GOLDEN TOUCH," CHANGED
THE MARKET CAP OF WASTE MANAGEMENT, AN ATLANTA-BASED TRASH
COMPANY, FROM $5 MILLION UPON ACQUISITION TO $3 BILLION. HIS
SECOND PURCHASE, BLOCKBUSTER, WENT FROM A MARKET VALUE OF $32
MILLION TO $8.4 BILLION UNTIL HE SOLD IT IN 1994.]

The time to be toughest is when things are going the best.

• • •

Success or failure [of a businesss] depends on the attitudes of the employees.

DONALD KEOUGH

Former President
COCA-COLA

[DONALD KEOUGH WAS PRESIDENT OF COCA-COLA UNTIL HIS RETIREMENT IN 1993. HE IS A BOARD MEMBER OF THE H. J. HEINZ COMPANY, NATIONAL SERVICE INDUSTRIES AND THE WASHINGTON POST.]

THE C.E.O.'S LITTLE INSTRUCTION BOOK

Self-confidence is important.
Confidence in others
is essential.

WILLIAM A. SCHREYER

Former CEO
MERRILL LYNCH & CO., INC.

[WILLIAM SCHREYER RETIRED A FEW YEARS AGO AS A SUCCESSFUL
BUSINESSMAN. UNDER HIS LEADERSHIP, MERRILL LYNCH'S REVENUES
SKYROCKETED AND ITS STOCKS QUADRUPLED IN THE EARLY 1990S.]

Motivation will always beat mere talent.

NORMAN R. AUGUSTINE

CEO
MARTIN MARIETTA CORP.

[PRIOR TO JOINING THE MARTIN MARIETTA CORPORATION, NORMAN WORKED FOR THE DEPARTMENT OF DEFENSE AND HELD FIVE POSITIONS AT ASSISTANT AND UNDERSECRETARY LEVELS. HE IS A MEMBER OF THE BOARDS OF DIRECTORS OF PHILLIPS PETROLEUM CO., RIGGS NATIONAL CORP. AND PROCTER AND GAMBLE CO.]

If you put fences around people,
you get sheep.

LIVIO DeSIMONE

CEO
3M

[LIVIO STARTED WORKING FOR **3M** STRAIGHT OUT OF COLLEGE. HE MADE
HIS WAY THROUGH THE RANKS AND EVENTUALLY BECAME **CEO**.]

*Exceed your customers' expectations...Give them wha[t]
they want — and a little more.*

• • •

*There is only one boss: the customer. And he can fire
everybody in the company, from the chairman on
down, simply by spending his money somewhere else[.]*

SAM WALTON

Founder
WAL-MART STORES

[SAM WALTON LEARNED THE VALUED PRINCIPLE OF CUSTOMER SATISFACTION EARLY IN HIS CAREER AS
A RETAILER. WITH IT, HE BUILT A FIVE-AND-DIME STORE INTO THE WORLD'S
LARGEST RETAIL COMPANY.]

Keep an open attitude and be willing to try new things.

ARTHUR C. MARTINEZ

CEO

SEARS ROEBUCK

[ARTHUR IS CREDITED WITH THE MAJOR OVERHAUL OF SEARS, CLOSING 113 UNPROFITABLE STORES; SHUTTING DOWN THE CATALOG DIVISION; AND MAKING IT A MORE APPEALING STORE FOR ITS TARGET CUSTOMERS, WOMEN. SEARS LOST $3.9 BILLION IN 1992, BUT UNDER THE FIRST YEAR OF ARTHUR'S GUIDANCE, EARNED OVER $1 BILLION.]

Don't sit down and wait for opportunities to come... Get up and make them!

MADAM C. J. WALKER

Founder
MADAM C. J. WALKER MANUFACTURING COMPANY

[WALKER WAS BORN "SARAH BREEDLOVE," THE DAUGHTER OF FORMER SLAVES. MARRIED AT FOURTEEN AND WIDOWED AT TWENTY, SHE DREAMED OF A BETTER LIFE FOR HER AND HER DAUGHTER. SHE INVENTED A HAIR CARE PRODUCT WHICH TOOK THE INDUSTRY BY STORM. IN 1917 SARAH WAS CONSIDERED NEW YORK'S WEALTHIEST BLACK WOMAN.]

With [creativity] most challenges can be met. Without it, problems are seldom converted into opportunities.

DAVID FAGIN

Chairman
GOLDEN STAR RESOURCES, LTD.

[IN 1992, AMERICAN GOLDFIELDS, INC. AND GOLDEN STAR RESOURCES, LTD. MERGED. THEY NEEDED AN ABLE LEADER WHO WAS EXPERIENCED AND REPUTABLE TO HEAD THEIR NEWLY ORGANIZED COMPANY. THEY FOUND THIS LEADERSHIP IN DAVID. PRIOR TO JOINING GOLDEN STAR, DAVID WAS PRESIDENT OF HOMESTAKE MINING CO.]

*Success is achieved through making a decision,
making it yours, and dying by it.*

• • •

*Don't spend your life trying to make right
decisions; invest your life making decisions
and making them right.*

CHARLES "TREMENDOUS" JONES

President
LIFE MANAGEMENT SERVICES, INC.

[CHARLIE JONES, FOUNDER OF HIS OWN MANAGEMENT COMPANY, SPECIALIZES IN GIVING MANAGEMENT
SEMINARS THROUGHOUT THE U. S. HE IS ALSO A RENOWNED WRITER AND SPEAKER.]

THE C.E.O.'S LITTLE INSTRUCTION BOOK

Success comes from a constant focus on renewal.

GARY TOOKER

CEO
MOTOROLA

[GARY, A GRADUATE OF ARIZONA STATE UNIVERSITY, JOINED MOTOROLA IN 1962. HE STARTED IN THE SEMICONDUCTOR SECTION OF THE COMPANY AND STEADILY WORKED HIS WAY UP TO TOP EXECUTIVE.]

The most important thing in the Olympic games is not winning but taking part...The essential thing in life is not conquering but fighting well.

BARON PIERRE DE COUBERTIN

Founder & First President
INTERNATIONAL OLYMPIC COMMITTEE

[IN 1894, BARON PIERRE DE COUBERTIN SET OUT TO RE-CREATE THE ANCIENT GREEK OLYMPICS AS A MEANS TO PROMOTE INTERNATIONAL FELLOWSHIP AND PROFICIENCY IN SPORTS. THE OLYMPIC GAMES TODAY IS AN INTERNATIONAL EVENT THAT DRAWS THOUSANDS OF ATHLETES FROM ALL OVER THE WORLD.]

Leaders get results through people.

PATRICIA FRIPP

Former President
NATIONAL SPEAKERS' ASSOCIATION

[PATRICIA BEGAN HER CAREER IN HAIRSTYLING AT AGE 15 IN ENGLAND, LATER MOVING TO SAN FRANCISCO WITH ONLY $500 IN HER POCKET. PATRICIA BEGAN BUILDING HER CLIENTLELE AND, THREE YEARS LATER SHE WAS ONE OF THE FIRST WOMEN WORKING IN THE MEN'S HAIRSTYLING PROFESSION. TODAY SHE RUNS A VERY SUCCESSFUL SALON AND PRODUCT DISTRIBUTION BUSINESS.]

Success does not come to you. You go to it.

• • •

If it is to be, it is up to me.

WALLY AMOS

Founder
FAMOUS AMOS

[WHEN WALLY WAS TWELVE, HE LEFT FLORIDA TO LIVE WITH HIS AUNT DELIA IN NEW YORK. SHE INTRODUCED HIM TO HOMEMADE CHOCOLATE CHIP COOKIES. AT THE SUGGESTION OF B. J. GILMORE, QUINCY JONES' SECRETARY, WALLY, WHO PLANNED A CAREER IN ENTERTAINMENT, BEGAN A COOKIE BUSINESS WHICH IS THRIVING TODAY.]

The customer is the boss.

DAVID GLASS

CEO

WAL-MART

[GLASS HAS ENGINEERED NUMEROUS INNOVATIONS, KEEPING WAL-MART
AT THE FOREFRONT OF THE RETAILING INDUSTRY. HIS STRATEGIES INCLUDE
OPENING DISCOUNT STORES AND SAM'S CLUBS SIDE BY SIDE TO EXPLOIT
THE MARKETING SYNERGY BETWEEN BOTH CONCEPTS.]

...Hire people who are more talented than [you] are.

STEVEN LEEBOW

Founder and CEO
PACESETTER STEEL

[STEVEN FOUNDED PACESETTER STEEL IN 1977. SINCE 1983, IT HAS BEEN ON THE FORTUNE 500 LIST, MAKING AN EXCESS OF OVER $100 MILLION DOLLARS IN SALES. ONE OF PACESETTER'S COMPETITORS IS MAJESTIC STEEL SERVICE, A COMPANY FOUNDED BY STEVEN'S YOUNGER BROTHER, DENNIS.]

It is only as we develop others
that we permanently succeed.

HARVEY S. FIRESTONE

Founder

FIRESTONE TIRE & RUBBER COMPANY

[IN 1900, HARVEY FORMED THE FIRESTONE TIRE & RUBBER COMPANY
AND WAS PRESIDENT UNTIL 1932. FIRESTONE STARTED OFF AS THE MAIN
SUPPLIER OF TIRES FOR FORD MOTOR COMPANY, BECOMING A MAJOR,
NATIONAL SUPPLIER OF TIRES BY THE 1930S.]

Honesty is the cornerstone of all success.

• • •

*Recognition is the most powerful of all motivators.
Even criticism can build confidence when it's
"sandwiched" between layers of praise.*

MARY KAY ASH

Founder
MARY KAY COSMETICS

[MARY KAY STARTED HER COSMETICS COMPANY WITH HER SON, RICHARD, NOW CHAIRMAN OF THE
MILLION DOLLAR COMPANY. THE COMPANY'S PHENOMENAL SUCCESS IS CREDITED TO MARY KAY'S
ABILITY TO MOTIVATE HER SALES FORCE TO MARKET HER PRODUCTS. TODAY, SHE REMAINS ACTIVE IN
THE COMPANY AS CHAIRMAN EMERITUS.]

THE C.E.O.'S LITTLE INSTRUCTION BOOK

*Don't lose sleep over problems
that may go away.*

RICHARD JENRETTE

Co-founder
DONALDSON, LUFKIN & JENRETTE

[WHEN DICK JENRETTE CO-FOUNDED DONALDSON, LUFKIN & JENRETTE
(DLJ), A WALL STREET FIRM, HE WAS INSTALLED AS CEO DURING A
RECESSION THAT PUT MOST WALL STREET FIRMS OUT OF BUSINESS.
UNDER HIS LEADERSHIP DLJ SURVIVED, AND DICK REMAINED CEO UNTIL IT
WAS BOUGHT BY EQUITABLE IN 1985.]

The will to persevere is often the difference between failure and success.

DAVID SARNOFF

Founder
NBC

[DAVID PIONEERED THE DEVELOPMENT OF THE FIRST "RADIO MUSIC BOX" IN
1916, WHICH BECAME VERY POPULAR AFTER AN AUDIENCE OF OVER
300,000 TUNED IN TO HIS BROADCAST OF THE DEMPSEY-CARPENTIER
BOXING MATCH. BY 1930, HE BECAME PRESIDENT OF RCA, SET UP AN
EXPERIMENTAL TELEVISION STATION AND FOUNDED NBC.]

There's no telling how far a person can go if he's willing to let other people take the credit.

ROBERT WOODRUFF

Former CEO
COCA-COLA

[AFTER ERNEST WOODRUFF BOUGHT COCA-COLA, HE HIRED HIS SON ROBERT TO RUN IT. ROBERT MADE COCA-COLA AN INTERNATIONAL HOUSEHOLD NAME.]

Leadership is practiced not so much in words as in attitude and in actions.

• • •

What you manage in business is people.

HAROLD GENEEN

CEO
ITT

[HAROLD GENEEN FORGED HIS REPUTATION AS A TOUGH-MINDED ACCOUNTANT WITH AN IMPRESSIVE RECORD AT JONES & LAUGHLIN, BELL & HOWELL, AND RAYTHEON BEFORE HE TOOK OVER ITT. HE MASTERMINDED ITT'S TREMENDOUS SUCCESS IN THE 1960S AND 70S, MOVING ITT FROM GROSSING LESS THAN $800 MILLION ANNUALLY TO $22 BILLION.]

Productivity is the name of the game...

WILLIAM HEWLETT

Co-founder
HEWLETT PACKARD

[BILL HEWLETT AND DAVID PACKARD CREDIT MUCH OF THEIR DRIVE AND INSPIRATION TO A STANFORD COLLEGE PROFESSOR, FREDERICK A. TERMAN. WITH HIS SUPPORT, THE TWO MEN BEGAN HEWLETT PACKARD IN DAVE'S GARAGE. THEIR FIRST MAJOR CUSTOMER WAS THE WALT DISNEY COMPANY.]

When you're building mountains, it's best not to look at those God has already made.

RON TOOMER
President
ARROW DYNAMICS

[WHEN ARROW DYNAMICS WANTED TO RE-ENTER THE ROLLER-COASTER BUSINESS, IT LOOKED TO RON AS ITS FIRST ENGINEER. TODAY, UNDER RON'S LEADERSHIP, ARROW DYNAMICS IS THE PRINCIPAL ROLLER-COASTER BUILDER IN THE WORLD.]

Consumers are statistics.
Customers are people.

STANLEY MARCUS

Chairman Emeritus
NEIMAN-MARCUS

[STANLEY TOOK OVER NEIMAN-MARCUS, FOUNDED BY HIS FATHER, UNCLE
AND AUNT IN 1907, AND MADE IT A SUCCESSFUL BUSINESS THAT IS
SYNONYMOUS WITH TASTEFUL, UPSCALE SHOPPING.]

*Fear of failure must never be a reason
not to try something.*

• • •

*Leadership is both something you are,
and something you do.*

FREDERICK SMITH

Founder
FEDERAL EXPRESS

[WHEN CONTRACT NEGOTIATIONS WITH THE FEDERAL RESERVE SYSTEM FELL THROUGH, FRED SMITH CREATED FEDERAL EXPRESS. ALTHOUGH SUCCESS DIDN'T COME OVERNIGHT, BY 1983 FEDERAL EXPRESS BECAME THE FASTEST COMPANY TO REACH A BILLION DOLLARS IN REVENUE.]

THE C.E.O.'S LITTLE INSTRUCTION BOOK

The real secret of success is enthusiasm. Yes, more than enthusiasm, I say excitement. I like to see men get excited. When they get excited they make a success of their lives.

WALTER P. CHRYSLER

Founder

CHRYSLER CORPORATION

[WALTER BEGAN HIS CAREER IN THE AUTO INDUSTRY AS A MACHINIST. HE QUICKLY ROSE THROUGH THE RANKS AND, BY 1916, HAD BECOME PRESIDENT OF BUICK MOTOR COMPANY, A DIVISION OF GENERAL MOTORS. FIVE YEARS LATER, HE JOINED THE MAXWELL MOTOR COMPANY, WHICH IN 1925 BECAME THE CHRYSLER CORPORATION.]

Do common things uncommonly well.

HENRY J. HEINZ

Co-founder and President
H. J. HEINZ & CO.

[HENRY HEINZ IS A MANUFACTURER OF PREPARED FOODS WHO, WITH HIS BROTHER AND COUSIN, FOUNDED A PARTNERSHIP THAT BECAME THE H. J. HEINZ COMPANY. HEINZ BECAME PRESIDENT WHEN IT WAS INCORPORATED IN 1905.]

Accomplishment influences confidence, and confidence influences accomplishment.

HAROLD S. HOOK

Chairman
AMERICAN GENERAL CORP.

[HAROLD BEGAN WORKING FOR AMERICAN GENERAL AS PRESIDENT OF A SUBSIDIARY. IN 1975 HE WAS ELECTED PRESIDENT AND SUBSEQUENTLY TOOK OVER AS CHAIRMAN AND CEO. HAROLD IS SCHEDULED TO RETIRE IN OCTOBER, 1996.]

Eagles don't flock — you have to find them one at a time.

• • •

Any company that spends a lot of time on internal fighting will lose the battle against the competition.

H. ROSS PEROT

Founder
ELECTRONIC DATA SYSTEMS

[WHILE ROSS PEROT WAS STILL WORKING AT IBM, HE FOUNDED ELECTRONIC DATA SYSTEMS (EDS). BY THE TIME HE SOLD EDS TO GENERAL MOTORS IN 1984, IT WAS WORTH OVER $2 BILLION. FOUR YEARS LATER, PEROT RETURNED TO THE COMPUTER INDUSTRY AND FORMED THE PEROT SYSTEMS CORPORATION IN WASHINGTON, D.C.]

THE C.E.O.'S LITTLE INSTRUCTION BOOK

Procrastination is opportunity's natural assassin.

VICTOR KIAM

Former Chairman
REMINGTON PRODUCTS, INC.

[VICTOR WORKED FOR THREE YEARS WITH INTERNATIONAL LATEX CORPORATION AND FOR NINE YEARS AS OWNER OF BENRUS WATCH COMPANY, INC. BEFORE HE BOUGHT REMINGTON PRODUCTS.]

Credentials are not the same as accomplishments.

ROBERT HALF

President
ROBERT HALF INTERNATIONAL

[ROBERT IS FOUNDER AND PRESIDENT OF ROBERT HALF INTERNATIONAL, A HIGHLY SUCCESSFUL RECRUITING FIRM WITH OFFICES IN THREE CONTINENTS. HE IS AUTHOR OF THE BESTSELLER, *THE ROBERT HALF WAY TO GET HIRED IN TODAY'S JOB MARKET.*]

Perceptions may count in the short term, but substance always prevails.

BARBARA CAPSALIS

Senior Vice President
CHEMICAL BANK OF NEW YORK

[WHEN BARBARA GRADUATED FROM COLLEGE, SHE HAD A CLEAR PLAN FOR HER LIFE: WORK ONE TO TWO YEARS, GET MARRIED AND LIVE HAPPILY EVER AFTER. TODAY, SHE IS STILL MARRIED AND STILL WORKING. BARBARA IS RESPONSIBLE FOR THE BANK'S NON-CREDIT SERVICES WORLDWIDE AND MANAGES 2,500 PEOPLE.]

*A leader is...someone who carries water for his
people so that they can get on with their jobs.*

• • •

If you don't do it excellently, don't do it at all.

ROBERT TOWNSEND

Former President
AVIS

[ROBERT IS A FORMER DIRECTOR OF AMERICAN EXPRESS. WHEN HE ASSUMED LEADERSHIP IN AVIS,
HE ENGINEERED A MAJOR TURNAROUND THAT BROUGHT THE COMPANY INTO THE BLACK FOR THE FIRST
TIME IN THIRTEEN YEARS. CURRENTLY, ROBERT IS AN AUTHOR AND RENOWNED SPEAKER.]

THE C.E.O.'S LITTLE INSTRUCTION BOOK

Problems are only opportunities in work clothes.

HENRY J. KAISER

Founder
KAISER INDUSTRIES

[HENRY KAISER OPENED HIS HEALTH CARE BUSINESS WHEN HE REALIZED THAT, WITH THE CLOSE OF WORLD WAR II, HIS SHIPBUILDING OPERATION WAS GOING TO GO UNDER. AS OF 1990, KAISER HAD 6.5 MILLION MEMBERS IN SIXTEEN STATES.]

Never think a job is more than you can do. Your potential is unlimited if you just put your mind to it.

PATRICIA LINDH

Vice President, Wholesale Marketing
BANK OF AMERICA

[SEVEN YEARS AFTER PATRICIA RETIRED AND MARRIED, SHE BECAME THE LIAISON WITH WOMEN'S ORGANIZATIONS DURING NIXON'S ADMINISTRATION, THE SPECIAL ASSISTANT FOR WOMEN UNDER FORD'S ADMINISTRATION, AND LATER THE DEPUTY ASSISTANT SECRETARY OF STATE FOR EDUCATIONAL AND CULTURAL AFFAIRS.]

An environment of uncertainty produces a lot of fear.

ROBERT HAAS

CEO
LEVI STRAUSS & COMPANY

[ROBERT IS THE GREAT-GREAT-GRANDNEPHEW OF LEVI STRAUSS, FOUNDER OF THE COMPANY. AT THE HELM, ROBERT HAS MAINTAINED THE SUCCESS OF THE COMPANY AS THE WORLD'S LARGEST APPAREL MAKER.]

Experience, if it doesn't kill you,
teaches you how to bounce back.

• • •

Success is not so much achievement as achieving.

DAVID J. MAHONEY

Founder
BANYAN SYSTEMS INC.

[IN 1983, AFTER ELEVEN YEARS WITH DATA GENERAL, DAVID FORMED BANYAN SYSTEMS, A COMPANY AIMED AT PROVIDING NETWORK OPERATING SYSTEMS TO BUSINESSES. TODAY, BANYAN SYSTEMS COMMANDS ALMOST HALF OF THE U. S. MARKET.]

THE C.E.O.'S LITTLE INSTRUCTION BOOK

There may be luck in getting a job, but there's no luck in keeping it.

J. OGDEN ARMOUR

Former President
ARMOUR MEAT PACKING COMPANY

[J. OGDEN ARMOUR INHERITED HIS FATHER'S MEAT-PACKING COMPANY, ARMOUR AND COMPANY, AND BUILT IT INTO THE WORLD'S LARGEST MEAT-PACKING INDUSTRY.]

My formula for success? Rise early, work late, strike oil.

JEAN PAUL GETTY

Founder
GETTY OIL CO.

[J. PAUL GETTY MADE HIS FIRST MILLION AT THE AGE OF TWENTY-THREE WHEN HE ENTERED THE OIL BUSINESS IN OKLAHOMA. HE STARTED THE GETTY OIL COMPANY AND WAS CONSIDERED THE RICHEST MAN IN THE WORLD BY 1957.]

You have to believe in the impossible.

HOWARD HEAD

Founder
HEAD SKIS
PRINCE TENNIS

[HOWARD HEAD REVOLUTIONIZED TWO INDUSTRIES SIMPLY BECAUSE HE WANTED TO IMPROVE HIS ABILITIES. HIS INVENTIONS PROVED SO SUCCESSFUL THAT HEAD SKIS AND PRINCE TENNIS ARE NOW THE STATUS SYMBOLS OF THEIR RESPECTIVE SPORTS.]

*The key to successful leadership
...is influence, not authority.*

• • •

Serve your people and help them win....

KENNETH H. BLANCHARD

Co-founder and Chairman
BLANCHARD TRAINING & DEVELOPMENT

[KEN, A SOUGHT-AFTER SPEAKER AND BUSINESS CONSULTANT, HAS WRITTEN SEVERAL BOOKS ON MANAGEMENT, INCLUDING THE BEST-SELLING *ONE MINUTE MANAGER*. CURRENTLY, HE HOLDS A FACULTY POSITION IN LEADERSHIP AT THE UNIVERSITY OF MASSACHUSETTS AND A VISITING LECTURESHIP AT CORNELL UNIVERSITY.]

Work is the basis of living...
A man will rust out quicker
than he'll wear out.

COLONEL HARLAND SANDERS

Founder
KENTUCKY FRIED CHICKEN

[WHILE MOST PEOPLE RETIRE AT AGE SIXTY-FIVE, COLONEL SANDERS WAS
TRAVELING AROUND IN HIS CAR, TRYING TO SELL HIS SECRET RECIPE FOR
FRIED CHICKEN. AND WITH THAT RECIPE, HE BUILT A MULTI-MILLION
DOLLAR FOOD FRANCHISE, KENTUCKY FRIED CHICKEN.]

It is well to think well; it is divine to act well.

HORACE MANN

President
ANTIOCH COLLEGE

[BEFORE HE ENTERED POLITICS, HORACE MANN PRACTICED LAW IN MASSACHUSETTS. HE WAS ELECTED STATE SENATOR AND KEPT HIS SEAT UNTIL HE WAS APPOINTED SECRETARY TO THE BOARD OF EDUCATION IN 1837. THROUGH HIS EFFORTS, THE PUBLIC SCHOOL SYSTEM ENJOYED DRAMATIC IMPROVEMENTS.]

Unless you're going to be a violinist or something, your success will...depend on other people.

WILLIAM G. MCGOWAN

Founder and Former Chairman
MCI COMMUNICATIONS CORP.

[THROUGH HIS TIRELESS LOBBYING IN WASHINGTON, WILLIAM MCGOWAN, FOUNDER OF MCI, CAUSED A SERIES OF FCC REGULATORY DECISIONS, INCLUDING THE LANDMARK GRANT TO MCI TO OFFER COMPETITIVE SERVICES. MCI IS CURRENTLY THE SECOND LARGEST LONG DISTANCE CORPORATION IN THE WORLD.]

If you can dream it, you can do it. Remember, this whole thing was started by a mouse.

• • •

Without inspiration...we would perish.

WALT DISNEY

Founder
WALT DISNEY CORPORATION

[WALT DISNEY LAUNCHED HIS DREAM OUT OF A GARAGE IN HOLLYWOOD BY DRAWING AND PERFECTING CARTOONS. WITH HIS NEW-FOUND SUCCESS IN CARTOON ANIMATION, HE CREATED THE WORLD'S FIRST ANIMATED FILM, "SNOW WHITE AND THE SEVEN DWARFS."]

Money is a very excellent servant, but a terrible master.

P. T. BARNUM

Co-founder
BARNUM & BAILEY'S CIRCUS

[BARNUM CONVERTED A MUSEUM IN NEW YORK CITY INTO A POPULAR ATTRACTION AND EVENTUALLY COMBINED THE MANY ELEMENTS INTO A HUGE CIRCUS, "THE GREATEST SHOW ON EARTH." TEN YEARS LATER, HE AND HIS CHIEF RIVAL JOINED FORCES AND BECAME "THE BARNUM & BAILEY CIRCUS."]

Groundless hope, like unconditional love, is the only kind worth having.

JOHN PERRY BARLOW

Vice Chairman
ELECTRONIC FRONTIER FOUNDATION

[WHEN JOHN LEFT THE CATTLE BUSINESS TO START A CAREER IN COMPUTERS, HE CO-FOUNDED ELECTRONIC FRONTIER FOUNDATION (EFF) WITH MITCHELL KAPOR, FORMER CEO OF LOTUS DEVELOPMENT CORP. EFF IS CURRENTLY THE LEADING PUBLIC-INTEREST GROUP WHOSE FOCUS IS ON CIVIL LIBERTIES IN THE WORLD OF ELECTRONIC COMMUNICATIONS.]

The new source of power is not money in the hands of a few but information in the hands of many.

JOHN NAISBITT

Chairman
NAISBITT GROUP

[JOHN IS A SOCIAL FORECASTER, SPEAKER, AND ADVISER TO MANY OF
AMERICA'S LEADING COMPANIES, SUCH AS AT&T, UNITED TECHNOLOGIES,
IBM, GENERAL ELECTRIC, AND CONTROL DATA. AN ENTREPRENEUR SINCE
1968, HE PREVIOUSLY WORKED FOR IBM, EASTMAN KODAK, AND THE
WHITE HOUSE.]

There is no substitute for hard work.

• • •

Good fortune is what happens when opportunity meets with preparation.

THOMAS A. EDISON

Inventor and Founder
EDISON ELECTRIC LIGHT COMPANY

[ALTHOUGH EDISON IS KNOWN FOR MANY INVENTIONS, HIS GREATEST CONTRIBUTION IS THE FIRST ELECTRIC LIGHT POWER STATION. ITS TREMENDOUS SUCCESS LED TO THE FOUNDING OF EDISON ELECTRIC LIGHT COMPANY, WHICH LATER MERGED INTO THE GENERAL ELECTRIC COMPANY.]

THE C.E.O.'S LITTLE INSTRUCTION BOOK

Goodwill is the one and only asset that competition cannot undersell or destroy.

MARSHALL FIELD

Founder
MARSHALL FIELD & CO.

[IN 1865, FIELD FOUNDED MARSHALL FIELD & CO., WHICH HE BUILT INTO A MILLION DOLLAR BUSINESS. HIS BUSINESS EXPANDED INTO A MANUFACTURING AND WHOLESALE MARKET. IN THE EARLY 1900S, FIELD ENTERPRISES FOUNDED THE CHICAGO SUN, LATER MERGED WITH THE SUN-TIMES, AND PUBLISHED THE WORLD BOOK ENCYCLOPEDIA.]

Think diversity. The idea of trying everything is important.

JILL ELIKANN BARAD
President
MATTEL, INC.

[JILL'S FIRST CHOICE OF OCCUPATION AS A DOCTOR FAILED WHEN SHE FAINTED DURING HER FIRST TIME IN AN OPERATING ROOM. THEN SHE TRIED ACTING AND LATER MOVED ON TO COSMETICS AND ADVERTISING. IN 1981 JILL BECAME THE PRODUCT MANAGER AT MATTEL WHERE SHE ENGINEERED BARBIE'S SUPERSTARDOM AS A VERSATILE CAREER WOMAN.]

Management's job is to see the company not as it is...but as it can become.

JOHN W. TEETS

CEO
DIAL CORPORATION

[WHEN JOHN ASSUMED THE LEADERSHIP ROLE AT DIAL CORPORATION, HE COMPLETELY OVERHAULED THE FAILING COMPANY. THROUGH HIS EFFORTS, DIAL CORPORATION IS ONCE AGAIN PROFITABLE, AND ITS STOCKS HAVE DOUBLED IN VALUE SINCE 1990.]

*If you want to succeed in business,
liberate other people's gifts.*

• • •

*The only thing that stands between a man
and what he wants from life is...the will to
try it and the faith to believe....*

RICHARD DEVOS

Co-founder and Former President
AMWAY CORPORATION

[RICH DEVOS, CO-FOUNDER OF AMWAY, ONE OF THE WORLD'S LARGEST PRIVATELY HELD COMPANIES,
RECENTLY RETIRED AS PRESIDENT. HE IS AN ACCLAIMED AUTHOR AND SPEAKER.]

The commitment to using the very best in all of us...is the umbrella over quality, customer satisfaction, profitability, efficiency — everything.

ALEX TROTMAN

CEO

FORD MOTOR COMPANY

[FOUR YEARS AFTER HIS DISCHARGE FROM THE ROYAL AIR FORCE, ALEX JOINED FORD-BRITAIN AND QUICKLY MOVED UP IN RANK, EVENTUALLY BECOMING PRESIDENT AND CHAIRMAN OF FORD OF EUROPE. IN 1993, ALEX TOOK OVER AS CHAIRMAN OF FORD MOTOR COMPANY. HE IS ALSO ON THE BOARD OF DIRECTORS FOR IBM CORPORATION.]

During my eighty-seven years, I have witnessed a whole succession of technological revolutions. But none of them has done away with the need for character in the individual or the ability to think.

BERNARD M. BARUCH

Chairman
WAR INDUSTRIES BOARD OF WORLD WAR I

[BERNARD MADE HIS CAREER AT WALL STREET IN A BROKERAGE HOUSE AND BECAME A PROSPEROUS YOUNG MAN. DURING WORLD WAR I, HE WAS APPOINTED CHAIRMAN OF THE WAR INDUSTRIES BOARD. HE WAS A DELEGATE AND ECONOMIC ADVISOR AT THE PARIS PEACE CONFERENCE, AND LATER SERVED AS ECONOMIC ADVISOR TO THE GOVERNMENT.]

Great successes are built on taking...a negative and turning it into a positive. Overcoming hazard. Overcoming danger. Overcoming catastrophe.

SUMNER REDSTONE

Chairman
VIACOM

[SUMNER OWNED A HIGHLY SUCCESSFUL THEATER CHAIN. BY THE AGE OF SIXTY-THREE, HE STARTED BUYING STOCKS IN A SMALL CABLE COMPANY. KNOWING VERY LITTLE ABOUT THE INDUSTRY, HE SET OUT TO LEARN WHAT HE COULD ABOUT IT. TODAY, REDSTONE IS A MAJOR CONGLOMERATE AND OWNER OF VIACOM, A MULTIBILLION DOLLAR COMPANY.]

Until you risk everything...
you're never going to lead.

• • •

Constructive criticism is never identified by the
mouth speaking, but by the ears listening.

DR. TOM HAGGAI

Chairman
INDEPENDENT GROCERS ALLIANCE (IGA)

[TOM HAS A DAILY RADIO SHOW CALLED "ONE MINUTE, PLEASE." DESPITE HIS BUSY SCHEDULE, HE
FINDS TIME TO GIVE MAJOR NATIONAL AND INTERNATIONAL ADDRESSES NEARLY EVERY WEEK.]

The only way you can measure character is by reputation.

ROBERTO GOIZUETA

CEO
COCA-COLA

[ROBERTO, A NATIVE OF CUBA, BEGAN WORKING FOR COCA-COLA AS A CHEMIST IN THE HAVANA PLANT. THROUGH HARD WORK AND DEDICATION, ROBERTO ADVANCED QUICKLY UP THE RANKS UNTIL HE WAS NAMED CHAIRMAN IN 1981. HE SERVES ON THE BOARDS OF DIRECTORS FOR SUNTRUST BANKS, INC., FORD MOTORS, AND EASTMAN KODAK.]

Satisfied employees are a necessary precondition for satisfied customers....

IRA STEPANIAN

Former CEO
BANK OF BOSTON

[IRA STEPANIAN STARTED HIS CAREER AS A MANAGEMENT TRAINEE. THROUGH HARD WORK, HE ROSE STEADILY TO HIGHER-LEVEL POSITIONS UNTIL HE WAS NAMED PRESIDENT IN 1983. AS PRESIDENT, HE SAVED THE BANK OF BOSTON FROM FINANCIAL DISASTER CAUSED BY A MOUNTAIN OF BAD LOANS.]

[Hire] outstanding people...
If [there is] a secret weapon,
this is it.

JAMES HENDERSON

CEO
CUMMINS ENGINE

[JAMES, A FORMER FACULTY MEMBER AT HARVARD BUSINESS SCHOOL, STARTED IN CUMMINS ENGINE AS AN ASSISTANT TO THE CHAIRMAN. HE WAS NAMED CHAIRMAN IN 1995. CURRENTLY, HE IS A TRUSTEE AT PRINCETON AND IS PRESIDENT OF THE TRUSTEES FOR CULVER EDUCATIONAL FOUNDATION.]

A problem well stated is a problem half solved.

• • •

Believe and act as if it were impossible to fail.

CHARLES F. KETTERING

Co-founder

SLOAN-KETTERING INSTITUTE FOR CANCER RESEARCH

[IN 1908, CHARLES KETTERING IMPROVED THE IGNITION SYSTEM THAT REVOLUTIONIZED THE AUTO INDUSTRY. FOUR YEARS LATER, THE CADILLAC DIVISION OF GENERAL MOTORS TURNED TO KETTERING'S NEW COMPANY FOR COMPONENTS THAT COMBINED IGNITION, LIGHTING, AND THE FIRST ELECTRIC SELF-STARTER.]

THE C.E.O.'S LITTLE INSTRUCTION BOOK

Do what you set out to do.

JOHN K. HANSON

Founder
WINNEBAGO INDUSTRIES, INC.

[IN THE LATE 1950s, JOHN SPEARHEADED A GROUP'S EFFORTS, PERSUADING MODERNISTIC INDUSTRIES TO BUILD A TRAVEL TRAILER MANUFACTURING PLANT IN FOREST CITY, IOWA. IN 1959, HANSON TOOK OVER THE PLANT. WHEN HE TOOK WINNEBAGO PUBLIC IN 1971, THE STOCK ROSE 462 PERCENT, MAKING TWO DOZEN LOCAL FOLKS MILLIONAIRES!]

Develop a product where there is no market — then create one.

AKIO MORITA
Co-founder
SONY

[ALTHOUGH AKIO'S BACKGROUND IS IN ENGINEERING, HE IS CREDITED FOR SONY'S SUCCESS AS HEAD OF WORLDWIDE SALES AND MARKETING. HE ALSO ENGINEERED THE PURCHASE OF CBS RECORDS AND COLUMBIA PICTURES, MAKING SONY A DOMINANT FORCE IN THE ENTERTAINMENT INDUSTRY.]

A career adventure is the better way to think about life.

ROGER ENRICO

CEO
PEPSICO

[IN 1971, ROGER BEGAN AT PEPSICO AS AN ASSOCIATE PRODUCTION MANAGER IN THE FRITO-LAY DIVISION. FROM THERE HE WORKED HIS WAY UP TO BECOME PRESIDENT OF PEPSICO FOODS JAPAN AND EVENTUALLY PRESIDENT OF PEPSICO, REPLACING CEO WAYNE CALLOWAY WHEN HE RETIRED IN APRIL, 1996.]

When the product is right, you don't have to be a great marketer.

• • •

You can have brilliant ideas, but if you can't get them across, your ideas won't get you anywhere.

LEE IACOCCA

Former Chairman
CHRYSLER CORPORATION

[IACOCCA BEGAN HIS CAREER IN THE AUTOMOBILE INDUSTRY WORKING FOR FORD MOTORS. HE MOVED UP THE CORPORATE LADDER AND EVENTUALLY BECAME PRESIDENT. AFTER BEING FIRED, HE JOINED THE FAILING CHRYSLER CORPORATION AND WITH HIS STRATEGIES, TURNED IT AROUND INTO A PROFOUNDLY LUCRATIVE BUSINESS.]

THE C.E.O.'S LITTLE INSTRUCTION BOOK

The great pleasure in life is doing what people say you cannot do.

WALTER BAGEHOT

Former Editor
THE ECONOMIST

[BAGEHOT'S ENDURING CLASSIC, *THE ENGLISH CONSTITUTION*, WRITTEN IN 1867, IS AN INSIGHTFUL ACCOUNT OF THE INNER WORKINGS OF THE BRITISH POLITICAL SYSTEM. HE WAS INSTRUMENTAL IN INTRODUCING THE TREASURY BILL, THE BANK RATE AND THE NOTION OF A CENTRAL BANK TAKING RESPONSIBILITY FOR THE VALUE OF A NATION'S CURRENCY.]

Time is the friend of the wonderful company, the enemy of the mediocre.

WARREN BUFFETT

CEO
BERKSHIRE HATHAWAY, INC.

[WARREN STARTED HIS CAREER WORKING AS AN INVESTMENT SALESMAN FOR HIS FATHER'S BROKERAGE FIRM. AT TWENTY-FIVE, WARREN FORMED BUFFET-PARTNERSHIP, A LIMITED PARTNERSHIP INVESTMENT FUND. IN 1969, HE TOOK OVER BERKSHIRE HATHAWAY, A SMALL TEXTILE COMPANY, WHICH CURRENTLY HAS HOLDINGS IN EXCESS OF $2 BILLION.]

Don't hold the penny so close to your eye that you can't see the dollar behind it.

MIKE MARKKULA

Co-founder and Chairman
APPLE COMPUTER

[MIKE IS A FORMER MARKETING EXECUTIVE AT INTEL. HE HELPED LAUNCH APPLE COMPUTER BY PROVIDING FINANCING AND SUPERVISION TO THE OTHER CO-FOUNDERS OF APPLE, STEVE WOZNIAK AND STEVE JOBS.]

Success or failure [of a business] depends on the attitudes of the employees.

• • •

The time to be toughest is when things are going the best.

DONALD KEOUGH

former President
COCA-COLA

[DONALD KEOUGH WAS PRESIDENT OF COCA-COLA UNTIL HIS RETIREMENT IN 1993. HE IS A BOARD
MEMBER OF THE H. J. HEINZ COMPANY, NATIONAL SERVICE INDUSTRIES, AND
THE WASHINGTON POST.]

*Life is about how you deal
with adversity.*

DIANA "DEDE" BROOKS

CEO
SOTHEBY'S

[DEDE'S CAREER WITH SOTHEBY'S BEGAN SEVENTEEN YEARS AGO, WHERE
SHE IMMEDIATELY CAUGHT THE ATTENTION OF ALFRED TAUBMAN, SOTHEBY'S
OWNER. UNDER HER LEADERSHIP, SOTHEBY'S HAS BECOME A WIDELY
RESPECTED AUCTION HOUSE. ONE OF THEIR MOST FAMOUS AUCTIONS WAS
THE RECENT JACKIE ONASSIS AUCTION.]

Winning organizations will be those that give individuals the chance to personally make a difference.

JOHN SCULLEY

Former CEO
APPLE COMPUTER CO.

[JOHN WAS A PEPSI MARKETER WHEN APPLE COMPUTER HIRED HIM AS CEO. WHEN HE LEFT APPLE COMPUTER, HE JOINED SPECTRUM TECHNOLOGIES. RECENTLY, KODAK RETAINED HIM AS A MARKETING ADVISOR TO HELP BUILD ITS DIGITAL IMAGING AND BRAND MARKETING STRATEGIES.]

The battle belongs to the persistent. Refuse to let friends or circumstances defeat you.

WILLIAM V. CROUCH

President
VAN CROUCH COMMUNICATIONS, INC.

[AFTER RANKING AS A SALES LEADER WITH THE AMERICAN EXPRESS COMPANY, VAN RECEIVED MANY AWARDS FOR OUTSTANDING PERFORMANCE IN THE INSURANCE INDUSTRY, BECOMING A MEMBER OF THE MILLION DOLLAR ROUND TABLE. HE IS THE AUTHOR OF SEVERAL BESTSELLERS AND IS ONE OF THE MOST VERSATILE SPEAKERS IN AMERICA.]

Ineffective leaders often act on the advice and counsel of the last person they talked to.

• • •

Leadership is the capacity to translate vision into reality.

WARREN G. BENNIS

Former President
UNIVERSITY OF CINCINNATI

[WARREN IS A DISTINGUISHED PROFESSOR OF BUSINESS ADMINISTRATION AT THE UNIVERSITY OF SOUTHERN CALIFORNIA. EARLIER HE SERVED AS PRESIDENT OF THE UNIVERSITY OF CINCINNATI AND AS CHAIRMAN OF ORGANIZATIONAL STUDIES AT THE MASSACHUSETTS INSTITUTE OF TECHNOLOGY'S SLOAN SCHOOL OF MANAGEMENT.]

When [people] work in a place that cares about them, they contribute a lot more than "duty."

DENNIS HAYES

CEO
HAYES MICROCOMPUTER PRODUCTS, INC.

[HAYES IS FOUNDER OF ONE OF THE FASTEST GROWING COMPANIES IN THE UNITED STATES. HE IS ALSO A MEMBER OF THE GEORGIA GOVERNOR'S ADVISORY COUNCIL ON SCIENCE AND TECHNOLOGY, WHICH KEEPS THE GOVERNOR AND LEGISLATURE ABREAST OF TECHNOLOGY AND SCIENCE ISSUES.]

Ethics must begin at the top of an organization.

EDWARD L. HENNESSY, JR.

Former CEO
ALLIED SIGNAL, INC.

[EDWARD WAS CEO FOR ABOUT TWENTY YEARS UNTIL HIS RETIREMENT IN 1991.]

Develop confidence in yourself and act as if you have it until you do.

BARBARA KROUSE

Vice President
Product Development
STOUFFER FOODS CORPORATION

[BARBARA BEGAN HER CAREER WITH STOUFFER'S AS A RESEARCH ASSISTANT IN 1969. SHE WAS PROMOTED TO ASSISTANT MANAGER OF RESEARCH AND DEVELOPMENT AND LATER TO MANAGER. HER DESIRE FOR TASTY, NON-FATTENING, EASY-TO-FIX DINNERS BECAME THE BASIS FOR LEAN CUISINE, WHICH HAS REVOLUTIONIZED THE FROZEN DINNER INDUSTRY.]

Dismiss personal grudges promptly.

• • •

Tact is the personal ingredient that smoothes out the rough spots of life.

ALLAN J. HURST

President
QUORUM LTD.

[ALLAN IS A RENOWNED NATIONAL SPEAKER, BEST KNOWN FOR THE EDUCATIONAL PROGRAMS HE DEVELOPED FOR SALES, MARKETING AND MANAGEMENT. HE MEETS WITH OVER A HUNDRED GROUPS ANNUALLY AND IS THE RECIPIENT OF NUMEROUS AWARDS FROM VARIOUS TRADE AND PROFESSIONAL GROUPS.]

*All great companies have been
built by individuals.*

RUPERT MURDOCH

Chairman
NEWS CORPORATION

[UNDER NEWS CORPORATION, AN UMBRELLA FIRM FOR MURDOCH'S MEDIA
HOLDINGS, IS TWENTIETH CENTURY FOX, FOX TV AND FX CABLE
NETWORKS, TV GUIDE, NEW YORK POST AND NEW YORK MAGAZINE,
HARPERCOLLINS, A THIRD OF BRITAIN'S NEWSPAPERS AND HALF OF
AUSTRALIA'S, A TV SATELLITE NETWORK IN EUROPE AND ASIA, AND MCI.]

The people who get into trouble...are those who carry around the anchor of the past.

JOHN F. WELCH, JR.

CEO
GENERAL ELECTRIC

[AFTER JOHN WELCH RECEIVED HIS PH.D. IN CHEMICAL ENGINEERING FROM THE UNIVERSITY OF ILLINOIS, HE BEGAN HIS CAREER WITH GENERAL ELECTRIC. HE WORKED HIS WAY TO BECOMING CHAIRMAN OF THE COMPANY. GENERAL ELECTRIC IS CURRENTLY ENJOYING ITS GREATEST SUCCESS EVER UNDER JOHN'S LEADERSHIP.]

Persistence propels potential to perfection.

SOICHIRO HONDA

Founder
HONDA MOTOR COMPANY

[HONDA MOTOR COMPANY, STARTED WITH A MOTORCYCLE BUSINESS, WAS AN INSTANT SUCCESS. AFTER SECURING THE MOTORCYCLE INDUSTRY, HONDA WENT INTO THE AUTOMOBILE INDUSTRY. DESPITE THE HIGH FAILURE RATE IN THE INDUSTRY, HONDA MADE IT SUCCESSFULLY AND EVEN BURIED OTHERS IN HIS WAY.]

You have no greater leverage than the truth.

• • •

Good entrepreneurs are risk-avoiders, not risk-takers.

PAUL HAWKEN

Founder

SMITH & HAWKEN GARDENING TOOL CO.

[PAUL BUILT SMITH & HAWKEN, A MAIL ORDER GARDEN TOOL COMPANY, INTO A BUSINESS THAT GENERATES MILLIONS OF DOLLARS IN SALES. HE ALSO FOUNDED A NATURAL FOODS COMPANY. PAUL DETAILS HIS VAST BUSINESS EXPERIENCE AND KNOWLEDGE IN *GROWING A BUSINESS*, A "HOW-TO" BOOK ON STARTING AND MAINTAINING A BUSINESS.]

If [you] treat [your] employees correctly, they'll treat the customers right. And if customers are treated right, they'll come back.

J. W. MARRIOTT, JR.

Chairman

MARRIOTT CORPORATION

[BILL MARRIOTT IS CHAIRMAN OF MARRIOTT CORPORATION, THE PARENT COMPANY OF HOST MARRIOTT AND MARRIOTT INTERNATIONAL. HE IS ALSO A TRUSTEE FOR THE NATIONAL GEOGRAPHIC SOCIETY AND A MEMBER OF THE NATIONAL ADVISORY BOARD OF THE BOY SCOUTS OF AMERICA.]

In order to get experience you have to get knocked around... Experience, if it doesn't kill you, teaches you how to bounce back.

DAVID J. MAHONEY

Founder

BANYAN SYSTEMS, INC.

[AFTER ELEVEN YEARS WITH DATA GENERAL, IN 1983 DAVID FORMED BANYAN SYSTEMS, A COMPANY AIMED AT PROVIDING NETWORK OPERATING SYSTEMS TO BUSINESSES. TODAY, BANYAN SYSTEMS COMMANDS ALMOST HALF OF THE U. S. MARKET.]

Set your goals high and don't let anybody tell you no.

MURIEL SIEBERT

President
MURIEL SIEBERT AND COMPANY

[MURIEL WAS THE FIRST WOMAN TO HOLD A SEAT ON THE NEW YORK STOCK EXCHANGE. IN 1977 SHE BECAME THE SUPERINTENDENT OF BANKS FOR NEW YORK STATE. LATER, SHE WAS APPOINTED BY THE GOVERNOR OF NEW YORK TO REGULATE ALL OF THE BANKS IN THE STATE.]

The way people deal with things that go wrong is an indicator of how they deal with change.

• • •

Rely on your intuition.

WILLIAM GATES III

Founder
MICROSOFT CORP.

[BILL GATES FOUNDED MICROSOFT BY WRITING PROGRAMS FOR ONE OF THE EARLIER COMPUTER MODELS. WHEN GATES SECURED A CONTRACT FROM IBM TO CREATE AN OPERATING SYSTEM FOR THEIR PCS, MICROSOFT BECAME AN OVERNIGHT SUCCESS. GATES IS CONSIDERED THE YOUNGEST SELF-MADE BILLIONAIRE IN THE WORLD.]

Keep it cheap, keep it simple,
focus your energy.

HERB KELLEHER

Chairman
SOUTHWEST AIRLINES

[KELLEHER, A STUDENT OF MILITARY HISTORY, HAS USED HIS KNOWLEDGE
OF MILITARY STRATEGIES IN HIS BUSINESS DEALINGS. HE CREDITS HIS
SOCIAL AND ECONOMIC EQUALITY VIEWS TO THE SUMMERS HE SPENT
WORKING ON THE FACTORY FLOOR OF CAMPBELL SOUP COMPANY,
MANAGED BY HIS FATHER.]

Never underestimate a hungry, purposeful, committed company.

ECKHARD PFEIFFER

CEO
COMPAQ

[ECKHARD TOOK OVER COMPAQ DURING A CRISIS. AS A RESULT OF
ECONOMY MEASURES WITH THE WORK FORCE, DEALERS, AND SUPPLIERS
AND OPENING 24-HOUR MAIL-ORDER AND CUSTOMER-SERVICE PHONE LINES,
COMPAQ BECAME THE WORLD'S TOP PC VENDOR IN 1994.]

Serve the customer. Serve the customer. Serve the customer.

BERNARD MARCUS

Co-founder and CEO
HOME DEPOT

[BERNIE IS A FORMER PRESIDENT OF ODELL, INC. AND VICE PRESIDENT OF HANDY DAN HOME IMPROVEMENT. HIS ENTREPRENEURIAL SPIRIT DROVE HIM TO CO-FOUND HOME DEPOT, INC. WITH A FRIEND, ARTHUR BLANK. TODAY, HOME DEPOT ENJOYS FINANCIAL SUCCESS BY UTILIZING WAL-MART'S STRATEGY OF LOW PRICES AND HIGH VOLUME.]

Nothing so conclusively proves a man's ability to lead others as what he does from day to day to lead himself.

• • •

You have to have your heart in the business and the business in your heart.

THOMAS J. WATSON, SR.

Former President
IBM

[THOMAS STARTED ON HIS QUEST FOR SUCCESS WHEN HE MET CHARLES FLINT WHO HIRED HIM TO WORK FOR THE COMPUTING-TABULATING-RECORDING COMPANY (CTR), WHICH LATER BECAME INTERNATIONAL BUSINESS MACHINES (IBM). WHILE WORKING AT CTR, THOMAS BOUGHT SHARES IN THE COMPANY UNTIL HE BECAME THE MAJOR SHAREHOLDER.]

THE C.E.O.'S LITTLE INSTRUCTION BOOK

Never allow your sense of self to become associated with your sense of job. If your job vanishes, your self doesn't.

GORDON VAN SAUTER

Former President
CBS NEWS

[VAN SAUTER RECENTLY LEFT THE COMMERCIAL ARENA TO BECOME PRESIDENT AND GENERAL MANAGER OF KVIE, A PBS STATION IN SACRAMENTO, CALIFORNIA. VAN SAUTER IS A FORMER PRESIDENT OF CBS NEWS AND CBS SPORTS, AND FORMER EXECUTIVE OF FOX NEWS.]

Treat everyone by the same set of principles.

STEPHEN COVEY

Chairman
COVEY LEADERSHIP CENTER

[STEPHEN IS CHAIRMAN OF COVEY LEADERSHIP CENTER AND CHAIRMAN OF THE INSTITUTE FOR PRINCIPLE-CENTERED LEADERSHIP, A NON-PROFIT ORGANIZATION. HE HOLDS LEADERSHIP SEMINARS FOR TOP BUSINESS LEADERS WORLDWIDE. HE HAS A MBA FROM HARVARD AND A DOCTORATE FROM BRIGHAM YOUNG UNIVERSITY.]

Every addition to true knowledge is an addition to human power.

HORACE MANN

Founder and First President
ANTIOCH COLLEGE

[DURING HIS TENURE AS SECRETARY OF THE BOARD OF EDUCATION, HORACE VISITED EUROPEAN SCHOOLS WHERE HE STUDIED THEIR EDUCATIONAL CONDITIONS AND METHODS. UPON HIS RETURN, HE ADVOCATED THE ABOLITION OF CORPORAL PUNISHMENT, CAUSING A CONTROVERSY WHICH AROUSED PUBLIC SENTIMENT FOR SCHOOL REFORM.]

Hard work is the best investment a man can make.

• • •

The man who does not work for the love of work is not likely to...find much fun in life.

CHARLES SCHWAB

Former President
BETHLEHEM STEEL

[CHARLES STARTED WORK IN ANDREW CARNEGIE'S STEEL MILLS. HE WORKED HIS WAY UP INTO VARIOUS HIGH-LEVEL POSITIONS UNTIL HE WAS NAMED PRESIDENT OF CARNEGIE STEEL. HE BOUGHT BETHLEHEM STEEL COMPANY FROM ANDREW CARNEGIE AND EXPANDED HIS BUSINESS DURING WORLD WAR I.]

You are your first product....

PORTIA ISAACSON

Founder
FUTURE COMPUTING, INC.

[PORTIA IS A COMPUTER SCIENTIST AND FORMER MICROCOMPUTER STORE OWNER. SHE FOUNDED FUTURE COMPUTING, A PC INDUSTRY ANALYSIS FIRM, AND LATER SOLD IT TO MCGRAW-HILL. PORTIA IS CURRENTLY CHAIRMAN AND CEO OF INTELLISYS, A COMPANY SHE FOUNDED TO COMMERCIALIZE AN INTEGRATED HOME-CONTROL SYSTEM.]

Mistakes will be made, but...[these] are not so serious in the long run as the mistakes management makes if it is dictatorial.

WILLIAM L. MCKNIGHT

Founder
3M

[BORN ON A FARM IN SOUTH DAKOTA, WILLIAM'S FIRST BUSINESS TRANSACTION WAS WHEN HE TRADED A SHORT-LEGGED MILKING STOOL FOR THE BOOKKEEPER'S BENCH. ONE OF HIS SECRETS IN BUILDING A SUCCESSFUL COMPANY WAS EMPOWERING AND MOTIVATING HIS EMPLOYEES LONG BEFORE MOTIVATION ENTERED THE CORPORATE WORLD.]

When one door closes, another opens; but we often look so long and so regretfully upon the closed door that we do not see the one which has opened for us.

ALEXANDER GRAHAM BELL

Inventor and Former President
NATIONAL GEOGRAPHIC SOCIETY

[BELL WORKED ON THE IDEA OF TRANSMITTING SPEECH ELECTRONICALLY SINCE THE AGE OF EIGHTEEN. IN CREATING A MULTIPLE TELEGRAPH INSTRUMENT, HE CAME UP WITH THE IDEA OF A TELEPHONE. HIS INTRODUCTION OF THE FIRST TELEPHONE AT THE PHILADELPHIA CENTENNIAL EXPOSITION LED TO THE ORGANIZATION OF THE BELL TELEPHONE COMPANY.]

Support is "teamwork plus."

• • •

You build a business one customer at a time.

R. DAVID THOMAS
Founder and Senior Chairman
WENDY'S INTERNATIONAL

[DAVE THOMAS FOUNDED AND BUILT WENDY'S INTO A BILLION DOLLAR COMPANY. HE IS THE AUTHOR OF *WELL DONE*, A BOOK WITH STORIES FROM HIS LIFE AND THE LIVES OF OTHER SUCCESSFUL BUSINESS LEADERS, WHO BUILT THEIR BUSINESSES ON STRONG MORAL PRINCIPLES.]

THE C.E.O.'S LITTLE INSTRUCTION BOOK

To achieve your dream, you've got to dream about work.

PATRICIA GALLUP

Co-founder
PC CONNECTION

[PATRICIA AND HER PARTNER, DAVID HALL, FOUNDED PC CONNECTION IN 1982, STARTING WITH $8,000. DAVID BECAME THE COMPUTER ENGINEER AND PATRICIA BECAME THE MANAGER. PC CONNECTION IS CURRENTLY THE NATION'S LARGEST MAIL ORDER AND CATALOGUE PC AND PERIPHERALS COMPANY.]

Motivate [your people], train them, care about them and make winners out of them....

J. W. MARRIOTT, JR.

Chairman
MARRIOTT CORPORATION

[BILL MARRIOTT HAS WON NUMEROUS AWARDS FOR HIS SUCCESSFUL LEADERSHIP IN BUSINESS. IN THE 1980s, WHEN MARRIOTT WAS RIDDEN WITH DEBT AND FAILING, BILL STEPPED IN AND REORGANIZED THE ENTIRE CORPORATION. MARRIOTT IS ONCE AGAIN A PROFITABLE CORPORATION EARNING MILLIONS IN REVENUE.]

If a man goes into business with only the idea of making money, the chances are he won't.

JOYCE CLYDE HALL

Founder
HALLMARK CARDS, INC.

[JOYCE STARTED HALLMARK WITH HER TWO BROTHERS, ROLLIE AND WILLIAM. USING HER GIFTS AS AN INNOVATIVE MERCHANDISER, ADVERTISER AND CONSUMER RESEARCHER, SHE CAUSED ORIGINAL SENTIMENTS TO LITERALLY GO OUT OF STYLE. TODAY, HALLMARK CARDS ARE SYNONYMOUS WITH QUALITY AND STYLE IN GREETING CARDS.]

Growth is a by-product of the pursuit of excellence....

• • •

Devote 100% of your time to the critical issue.

ROBERT TOWNSEND

Former President
AVIS

[ROBERT, FORMER DIRECTOR OF AMERICAN EXPRESS, ENGINEERED A MAJOR TURNAROUND THAT BROUGHT AVIS INTO THE BLACK FOR THE FIRST TIME IN THIRTEEN YEARS. ROBERT IS CURRENTLY AN AUTHOR AND RENOWNED SPEAKER.]

To get rich today, you must help others get rich.

GEORGE PERRIN

Founder and Chairman
PAGE NET

[AFTER GRADUATING FROM THE UNIVERSITY OF MICHIGAN AND BUSINESS SCHOOL, GEORGE TOOK A JOB WITH THE NASCENT ELECTRONIC PAGING TRADE ASSOCIATION IN WASHINGTON, D.C. IN 1981, HE FORMED PAGE NET WHICH WENT PUBLIC IN 1991 AND HAS BECOME THE LARGEST PAGING NETWORK IN THE NATION.]

Stickability is 95 percent of ability.

DAVID J. SCHWARTZ

President
CREATIVE EDUCATIONAL SERVICES, INC.

[DR. SCHWARTZ IS A PROFESSOR AT GEORGIA STATE UNIVERSITY. HE IS
ALSO THE AUTHOR OF THE NATIONAL BESTSELLER,
THE MAGIC OF THINKING BIG.]

Learn to take risks and stretch beyond what you think your capabilities are.

ELLA MUSOLINO

President

SPORTS ETCETERA

[ELLA LAUNCHED SPORTS ETCETERA WHEN THE U. S. OPEN BECAME THE PREMIER EVENT IN TENNIS, BUT WAS NOT POPULAR ENOUGH TO GUARANTEE PRIZE MONEY OF $100,000. ELLA BEGAN CALLING CORPORATIONS. SPORTS ETCETERA NOW HANDLES BUDGETS IN EXCESS OF $1 MILLION FOR MERRILL LYNCH AND OTHER CLIENTS.]

Give me a stock clerk with a goal and I will give you a man who will make history. Give me a man without a goal and I will give you a stock clerk.

• • •

I will have no man work for me who has not the capacity to become a partner.

JAMES CASH PENNEY

Founder
J. C. PENNEY

[J. C. PENNEY WORKED FOR SEVERAL YEARS AT A DRY GOODS STORE IN COLORADO BEFORE HE BOUGHT THE BUSINESS. INITIALLY, HE BOUGHT A THIRD OF THE OPERATION AND EVENTUALLY BOUGHT OUT HIS PARTNERS. BY THE TIME OF HIS DEATH, J. C. PENNEY'S WAS THE COUNTRY'S FIFTH LARGEST MERCHANDISING COMPANY.]

Dare to be different.

AMELIA LOBSENZ

Chairman and CEO
LOBSENZ-STEVENS, INC.

[AMELIA BEGAN HER CAREER IN PUBLIC RELATIONS. EVENTUALLY SHE WAS INTRODUCED TO THE PUBLIC RELATIONS OFFICERS AT THE ROCKEFELLER BROTHERS FUND, AND WAS ASKED TO HANDLE PUBLIC RELATIONS ON THEIR REPORTS. TODAY, LOBSENZ-STEVENS, INC., HER OWN PUBLIC RELATIONS FIRM, HAS BILLINGS IN EXCESS OF $4 MILLION.]

There is usually a fantastic opportunity if you are tuned in to hear its knock.

MARY JO JACOBI

Corporate Vice President
Government and International Affairs
DREXEL BURNHAM LAMBERT, INC.

[MARY JO WAS AWARDED A TEACHING FELLOWSHIP AT GEORGE WASHINGTON UNIVERSITY. SHE BECAME THE NUMBER TWO LOBBYIST FOR 3M AND EVENTUALLY THE U. S. PRESIDENT'S LIAISON TO THE AMERICAN BUSINESS COMMUNITY. LATER, SHE BECAME CORPORATE VICE PRESIDENT FOR DREXEL BURNHAM LAMBERT, INC.]

I have a lot of things to prove to myself. One is that I can live fearlessly.

OPRAH WINFREY
HARPO PRODUCTIONS

OPRAH BEGAN HER CAREER IN TELEVISION AND RADIO. SHE BECAME THE FIRST BLACK AMERICAN WOMAN TO HOST A NATIONALLY SYNDICATED TALK SHOW, FOR WHICH SHE WAS AWARDED AN EMMY IN 1987. SHE IS ALSO THE FIRST BLACK AMERICAN WOMAN TO PURCHASE A TELEVISION AND FILM PRODUCTION STUDIO.]

Exhilaration of life can be found only with an upward look.

• • •

People come before product. First things first.

RICHARD M. DEVOS

Co-founder
AMWAY CORPORATION

[RICH DEVOS, CO-FOUNDER OF AMWAY, ONE OF THE WORLD'S LARGEST PRIVATELY HELD COMPANIES, RECENTLY RETIRED AS PRESIDENT. HE IS AN ACCLAIMED AUTHOR AND SPEAKER.]

To be a manager, you have to start at the bottom — no exceptions.

HENRY BLOCK

CEO
H&R BLOCK

[WHEN HENRY BLOCK STARTED H&R BLOCK, HIS ONLY TRAINING WAS IN MATHEMATICS AND BOOKKEEPING. HIS ONLY COMPETITION UNTIL THE EARLY 1990S WAS THE TAXPAYER WHO INSISTED ON FILLING OUT HIS/HER OWN TAX FORMS. CURRENTLY, H&R BLOCK IS A MILLION DOLLAR COMPANY AND REMAINS THE LEADER IN ITS INDUSTRY.]

*Feedback is the breakfast
of champions.*

KENNETH BLANCHARD

Chairman
BLANCHARD TRAINING & DEVELOPMENT

[KEN FOUNDED BLANCHARD TRAINING & DEVELOPMENT TO PROMOTE THE
PRINCIPLES HE ADVOCATES IN HIS BOOKS, SEMINARS, AND SPEECHES. HIS
CLIENT LIST READS LIKE A "WHO'S WHO" OF CORPORATIONS, ASSOCIATIONS,
AND INSTITUTIONS.]

The first step to achieving success is accepting the fact that nothing will ever replace hard work.

CLAIRE GARGALLI

President

EQUIBANK OF PITTSBURGH

[CLAIRE'S FIRST JOB WAS AT FIDELITY BANK IN PHILADELPHIA. AFTER BECOMING EXECUTIVE VICE PRESIDENT AND PRESIDENT, SHE WAS OFFERED THE POSITION OF SENIOR EXECUTIVE VICE PRESIDENT OF EQUIBANK AND WAS LATER PROMOTED TO PRESIDENT. CLAIRE IS THE HIGHEST RANKING FEMALE OFFICER OF ANY U. S. BANK.]

Identify...what you want for yourself and go for it.

MASAKO TANI BOISSONNAULT

Principal
ARCH-I-FORM, INC.

[MASAKO GRADUATED FROM TAMA FINE ARTS COLLEGE IN JAPAN AND ATTENDED THE ART CENTER COLLEGE OF DESIGN IN LOS ANGELES. SHE BECAME A DESIGN CONSULTANT, AND WORKED FOR SEVERAL FIRMS BEFORE STARTING HER OWN COMPANY. SHE HAS DONE WORK FOR SUCH CLIENTS AS DINER'S CLUB, TRW, AND CANDLE CORPORATION.]

Business is never easy, but the difficulties are not insurmountable.

EDGAR S. WOOLARD, JR.

CEO
DU PONT

[SINCE HE TOOK OVER AS CEO, EDGAR HAS BROUGHT ABOUT SIGNIFICANT CHANGES IN REORGANIZING DU PONT, TIGHTENING ITS BOTTOM LINE AND INCREASING ITS EFFICIENCY. AS A RESULT, DU PONT HAS SEEN SIGNIFICANT INCREASES, AND EDGAR HAS WON NUMEROUS PRESTIGIOUS AWARDS FOR HIS EFFORTS.]

Success comes from good judgment. Good judgment comes from experience.

ARTHUR JONES

Founder
NAUTILUS SPORTS/MEDICAL INDUSTRIES

[ARTHUR FOUNDED NAUTILUS BASED ON THE VARIABLE-RESISTANCE PRINCIPLES THAT REVOLUTIONIZED THE FITNESS TRAINING INDUSTRY. IN 1948, ARTHUR BUILT A PROTOTYPE AND LEFT IT IN THE TULSA YMCA WHERE HE WAS LIVING AT THE TIME. HE HAS BUILT MANY MORE PROTOTYPES AND LEFT THEM IN GYMS ALL AROUND THE WORLD.]

Love what you are doing and show it. Enthusiasm sells!

HELEN BOEHM

Chairman
EDWARD MARSHALL BOEHM, INC.

[HELEN BECAME ONE OF THE FIRST WOMEN IN NEW YORK LICENSED AS A DISPENSING OPTICIAN. AFTER SHE AND EDWARD MARRIED, THEY OPENED UP A BUSINESS TO MARKET ED'S PORCELAIN SCULPTURES. TODAY, BOEHM IS A WORLD LEADER IN FINE PORCELAIN WITH MANY PRESTIGIOUS CUSTOMERS.]

I'd rather have 1 percent of one hundred men's efforts than 100 percent of my own.

• • •

No one can possibly achieve any real and lasting success or get rich in business by being a conformist.

JEAN PAUL GETTY

Founder
GETTY OIL CO.

[J. PAUL GETTY MADE HIS FIRST MILLION AT THE AGE OF TWENTY-THREE WHEN HE ENTERED THE OIL BUSINESS IN OKLAHOMA. HE STARTED THE GETTY OIL COMPANY AND WAS CONSIDERED THE RICHEST MAN IN THE WORLD BY 1957.]

THE C.E.O.'S LITTLE INSTRUCTION BOOK

The moment you let avoiding failure become your motivator, you're [already headed] down the path of inactivity.

ROBERTO GOIZUETA

CEO
COCA-COLA

[WHILE ROBERTO WORKED AS AN ENTRY LEVEL CHEMIST AT THE COCA-COLA PLANT IN HAVANA, FIDEL CASTRO TOOK OVER CUBA AND ALL OF ITS BUSINESSES, INCLUDING HIS FAMILY'S SUGAR-REFINING BUSINESS. FORTUNATELY, ROBERTO HAD MOVED HIS ENTIRE FAMILY TO MIAMI BEFORE CASTRO'S TAKEOVER.]

*Credentials are not the same
as accomplishments.*

ROBERT HALF

President
ROBERT HALF INTERNATIONAL

[ROBERT HALF INTERNATIONAL IS CURRENTLY THE LARGEST PERSONNEL
SERVICE ORGANIZATION IN THE NATION. THIS COMPANY SPECIALIZES IN
PROVIDING PERSONNEL FOR ACCOUNTING, FINANCE, TAX, BANKING, AND
DATA PROCESSING FIELDS.]

I feel every person can have everything if they are willing to work, work, work.

ESTEE LAUDER
Founder
ESTEE LAUDER, INC.

[ESTEE LAUDER STARTED HER CAREER IN COSMETICS PEDDLING SKIN CREAMS HER UNCLE PRODUCED. A FEW YEARS LATER, SHE GOT A FOOTHOLD IN THE COSMETICS INDUSTRY WITH ONE TOP-SELLING PRODUCT. TODAY, ESTEE LAUDER IS A BILLION DOLLAR COMPANY WITH SEVERAL PRODUCT LINES SUCH AS CLINIQUE AND ARAMIS.]

To control your tongue is to control your very life.

• • •

... experience a turning point. Stay in the game — it's too soon to quit!

WILLIAM V. CROUCH

President
VAN CROUCH COMMUNICATIONS, INC.

[AFTER RANKING AS A CONSISTENT SALES LEADER WITH THE AMERICAN EXPRESS COMPANY, VAN WENT ON TO RECEIVE MANY AWARDS FOR OUTSTANDING PERFORMANCE IN THE INSURANCE INDUSTRY AND QUALIFIED AS A MEMBER OF THE MILLION DOLLAR ROUND TABLE. HE IS ONE OF AMERICA'S MOST VERSATILE SPEAKERS.]

THE C.E.O.'S LITTLE INSTRUCTION BOOK

*Bite off more than you can chew,
then chew it.*

ELLA WILLIAMS

Founder and CEO
FLETCHER ASSET MANAGEMENT

[IN 1981, ELLA STARTED HER DEFENSE CONTRACTING FIRM WITH A SMALL
BUSINESS ADMINISTRATION LOAN, HER CREDIT CARDS AND A SECOND
MORTGAGE ON HER HOUSE. ELLA FINALLY WON AN $8 MILLION CONTRACT
WITH THE NAVAL AIR WARFARE CENTER. SHE HAS SINCE WON NUMEROUS
PRESTIGIOUS AWARDS.]

Success...is simply the natural outcome of our directed intentions and actions.

IRA HAYES

Manager
Advertising Department
NCR CORPORATION

[IRA IS A FORMER PRESIDENT OF THE NATIONAL SPEAKERS' ASSOCIATION.
HE HAS GIVEN MANY SPEECHES AND HAS HELD POSITIVE THINKING RALLIES
THAT WERE ATTENDED BY THE THOUSANDS.]

Defeat is only a state of mind....

DAVID J. SCHWARTZ

President
CREATIVE EDUCATIONAL SERVICES, INC.

[DR. SCHWARTZ FOUNDED CREATIVE EDUCATIONAL SERVICES, A
CONSULTING FIRM THAT SPECIALIZES IN LEADERSHIP DEVELOPMENT. HE IS A
RENOWNED SPEAKER AND AUTHOR, WELL-KNOWN FOR HIS PROGRAM,
"SELF-DIRECTION FOR PERSONAL GROWTH."]

Work is the meat of life, pleasure the dessert.

• • •

There is more credit and satisfaction in being a first-rate truck driver than a tenth-rate executive.

B. C. FORBES

Founder
FORBES MAGAZINE

[B. C. FORBES STARTED *FORBES MAGAZINE* AS A BUSINESS PUBLICATION AIMED AT PROFILING BUSINESS LEADERS AND DISCUSSING MANAGEMENT POLICIES AND STYLES. UPON HIS DEATH, HIS SON MALCOLM TOOK OVER AND TURNED *FORBES MAGAZINE* INTO A SUCCESSFUL BUSINESS.]

Failure is not a fatal disease.

EARL G. GRAVES

Founder
BLACK ENTERPRISES

[GRAVES WAS A POLITICAL AIDE TO ROBERT F. KENNEDY. IN THE LATE 1960s, HE LEFT THE POLITICAL ARENA TO FULFILL A NEED HE SAW IN THE BLACK COMMUNITY: INVOLVEMENT IN BUSINESS AND GOVERNMENT. TODAY, BLACK ENTERPRISES IS A RAPIDLY GROWING EMPIRE AND AN INFLUENTIAL VOICE FOR MINORITY GROUPS.]

Information is power, and the gain you get from empowering your associates more than offsets the risk of informing your competitors.

SAM WALTON

Founder
WAL-MART STORES

[YOU WOULDN'T BE ABLE TO TELL THAT SAM WALTON WAS ONE OF THE RICHEST MEN IN AMERICA IF YOU MET HIM ON THE STREETS OF BENTONVILLE, ARKANSAS. DESPITE HIS FINANCIAL SUCCESS, HE STILL DROVE A PICKUP TRUCK, WORE A WAL-MART BALL CAP AND EVEN GOT HIS HAIR CUT AT THE SAME BARBER SHOP HE HAD FREQUENTED FOR YEARS.]

The path to success is to take massive, determined action.

ANTHONY ROBBINS

Founder and Chairman
ROBBINS RESEARCH INSTITUTE, INC.

[ANTHONY ROBBINS, A RENOWNED SPEAKER AND A BESTSELLING AUTHOR, HAS CONSULTED WITH CEOS, PROFESSIONAL SPORTS TEAMS, AND LEADERS FROM VARIOUS INDUSTRIES. HE HAS A SUCCESSFUL TV PROGRAM CALLED "PERSONAL POWER" AND IS THE FOUNDER OF NINE DIFFERENT COMPANIES.]

The three great essentials to achieve anything worthwhile are first, hard work; second, stick-to-itiveness; third, common sense.

• • •

Everything comes to him who hustles while he waits.

THOMAS A. EDISON

Inventor and Founder
EDISON ELECTRIC LIGHT COMPANY

[WHILE WORKING AS A TELEGRAPH OPERATOR, EDISON INVENTED A TELEGRAPH INSTRUMENT THAT ALLOWED MESSAGES TO BE TRANSMITTED ELECTRONICALLY OVER A SECOND LINE WITHOUT THE HELP OF AN OPERATOR. LATER, HE INVENTED A TELEGRAPH MACHINE THAT TRANSMITTED NUMEROUS MESSAGES SIMULTANEOUSLY ON ONE LINE.]

The common denominator for success is work.

JOHN D. ROCKEFELLER, JR.

Former President
STANDARD OIL COMPANY

[JOHN FINANCED THE ROCKEFELLER CENTER, MADE LARGE CONTRIBUTIONS TO THE LINCOLN CENTER AND HELPED RESTORE COLONIAL WILLIAMSBURG, VIRGINIA. HE EVEN ENGINEERED THE LOCATION OF THE UNITED NATIONS HEADQUARTERS IN THE UNITED STATES.]

ABOUT THE AUTHOR

Van Crouch is widely regarded as one of the best and more versatile speakers in America. As the founder and president of the consulting firm, *Van Crouch Communications, Inc.*, Van challenges individuals to achieve excellence in their lives.

Ranked as a consistent sales leader with the *American Express Company*, Van went on to receive many awards for outstanding performance in the insurance industry and has been a qualifying member of the *Million Dollar Round Table*.

Van Crouch authored the best-selling books, *Stay in the Game* and *Winning 101*, and is in demand for his thought-provoking seminars and keynote engagements to *Fortune 500* companies, government organizations, professional sports teams, church groups, as well as management and sales conventions worldwide.

Van Crouch has the ability to motivate people to raise their level of expectation. He is sure to both inspire and challenge you.

For more information about Van Crouch's seminars, speaking engagements, cassette tapes and videos, or to write the author, address your correspondence to:

Van Crouch Communications, Inc.
P. O. Box 320
Wheaton, IL 60189

Additional copies of this book and other titles in the *In The Midst of Greatness* Series, are available from your local bookstore.

The Presidents' Little Instruction Book

TRADE LIFE BOOKS, INC.
Tulsa, Oklahoma 74155